The story of Pinocchio

Illustrated by Mauro Evangelista

Retold by Katie Daynes
Based on the original story by Carlo Collodi

Gepetto the carpenter had always wanted to make a puppet. One day, he found the perfect piece of wood.

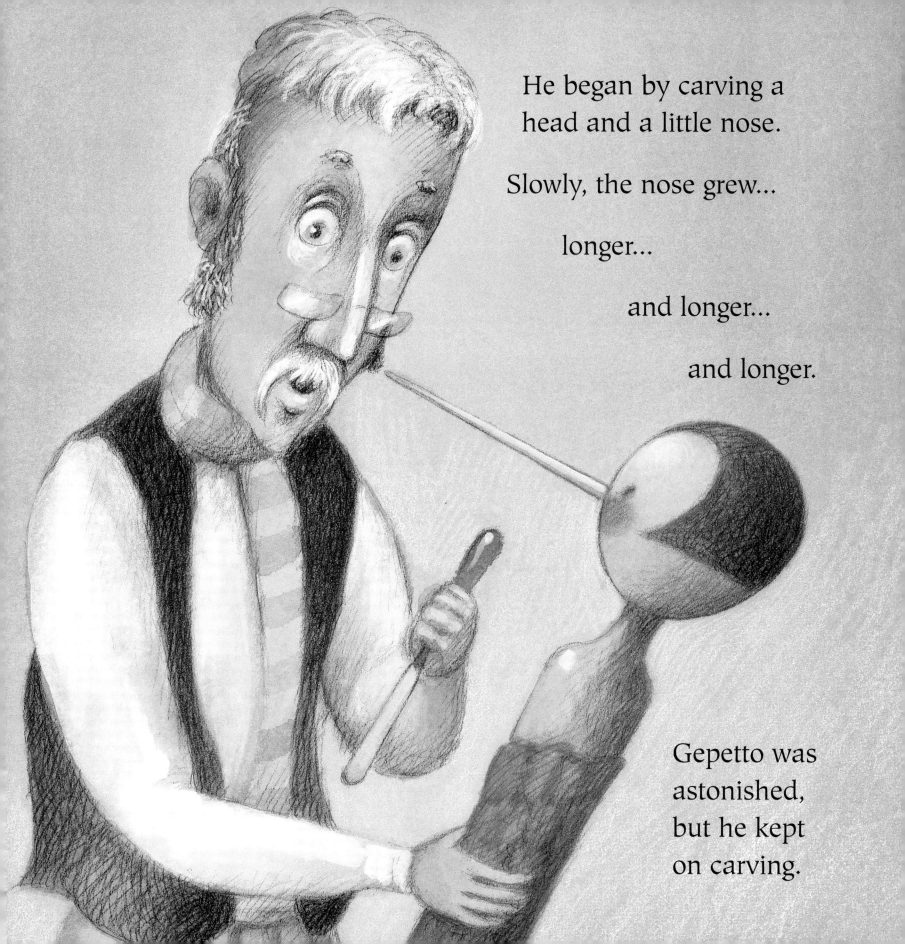

He began by carving a head and a little nose.

Slowly, the nose grew...

longer...

and longer...

and longer.

Gepetto was astonished, but he kept on carving.

Hours later, he finished his long-nosed puppet and smiled.

Suddenly, the puppet jumped up, snatched
Gepetto's wig and ran outside.

"Come back here, puppet!"
Gepetto cried.

"I'm not a puppet," shouted the puppet. "My name is Pinocchio and I'm a *real* boy."

Pinocchio kept running, straight past a policeman.

"What's going on?" asked the policeman.
Then he saw Gepetto waving a chisel.
"Stop there, old man," he ordered. "You look dangerous."

"Tee hee," giggled Pinocchio. He skipped back home and snuggled in an armchair by the fire.

buzzzzzzzzzzzzzzz

"Foolish puppet," buzzed a cricket.

"Hey!" shouted Pinocchio. "I'm
not a puppet. I'm a *real* boy."

"Oh no you're not," said
the cricket. "You're
a naughty puppet.
Only good puppets
become real boys."

Pinocchio was lost in thought...

until Gepetto arrived home with some supper.

"Er... Dad," said Pinocchio.
"I want to be a real boy."

Gepetto smiled.
"Well let's start by
sending you to school."

Be good, Pinocchio!

On the way to school, Pinocchio saw a crowd of people.

"Are you here for the puppet show?"
asked a well-dressed man.

"A puppet show?" said Pinocchio. "Oh yes!"

He sold his school book, bought a ticket...

...and dashed into the show.

"Hello puppet," the performers called to
Pinocchio. "Come and join us."

"We're going to the Land of Lost Toys," said a clown. "Do you want to come along?"

"I'd love to!" replied Pinocchio at once.

The Land of Lost Toys was one big funfair.

"Yippeeeeee!" squealed Pinocchio.

"Are you a lost toy too?"
asked a teddy bear.

"Um... yes," lied Pinocchio.
His wooden nose began to itch.

"I have no family," said the teddy bear.
"Nor do I," lied Pinocchio.

His itchy nose began to grow.

It grew

longer

and **longer**.

"Foolish puppet,"
buzzed a voice.
"You don't deserve
to be a real boy.
Your poor father is sick
with worry. He's rowing
across the ocean to find you."

"Oh no!" Pinocchio sighed. "I must
save him." Instantly, his nose began to shrink.

"I'll help you," cooed a pigeon.

Pinocchio jumped on her back
and they soared to the coast.

Pinocchio?
Where are you?

"There he is!"
cried Pinocchio.

As the puppet watched, a huge wave
rose up and swallowed Gepetto's boat.

"I'll save you, Dad!"
cried Pinocchio.

And he dived into the chilly water.

Pinocchio swam and swam... but there was no sign of Gepetto.

Then he felt a rush of water
and everything went dark.

"Where am I?" wondered Pinocchio, with a shudder.
Peering into the gloom, he saw a faint glow.

He followed it down a squelchy tunnel...

SQUELCH   SQUELCH

...and stopped in surprise.

An old man was sitting at a desk.
"Dad?" whispered Pinocchio.

Pinocchio!

"I'm sorry I was so naughty," said Pinocchio.
"But don't worry, I'll get us out of here."

Pinocchio led Gepetto back along the dark, squelchy tunnel, to the mouth of a cave.

"Jump!" cried Pinocchio. "I'll tow you to the shore."

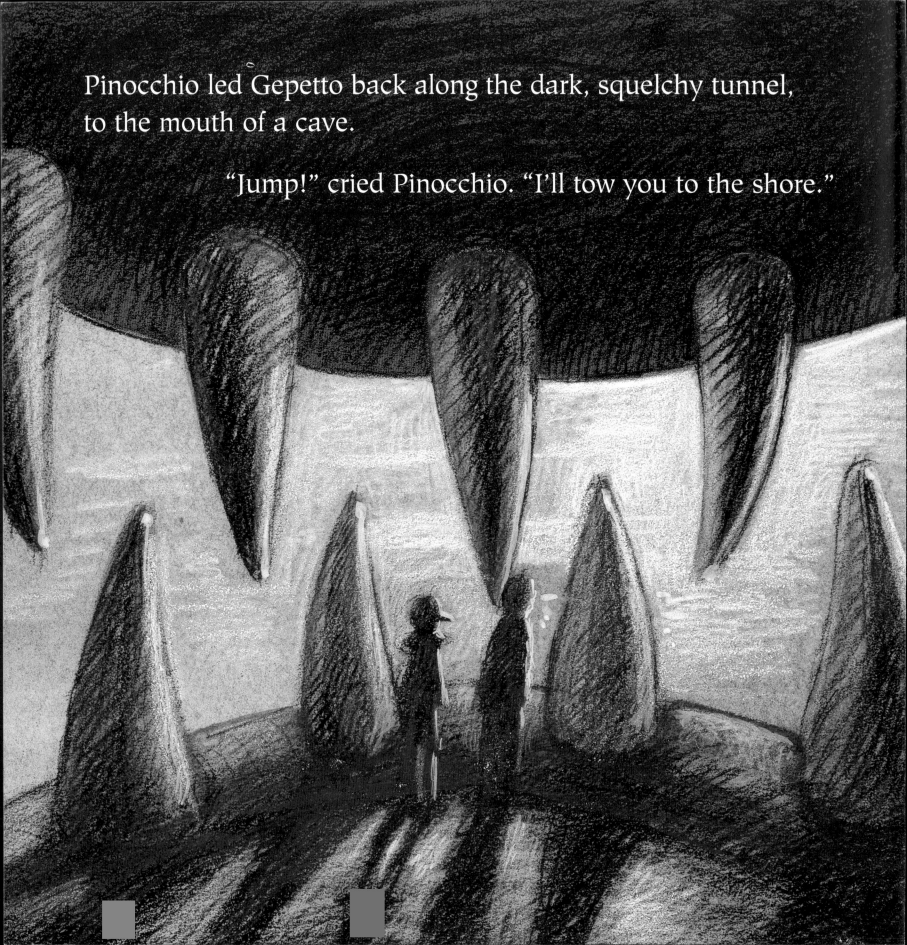

By midnight, Pinocchio and Gepetto were safely home.
"You're a good puppet," said Gepetto, kissing his son goodnight.

The next morning, Pinocchio woke
up feeling very different.

"Dad!" he
shouted. "I'm a
real boy at last."

Edited by Jenny Tyler and Lesley Sims
Designed by Andrea Slane and Katarina Dragoslavic
Cover design by Russell Punter

First published in 2005 by Usborne Publishing Ltd, 83-85 Saffron Hill, London EC1N 8RT, England.
www.usborne.com Copyright © 2005 Usborne Publishing Ltd. The name Usborne and the devices ♀ ⊕ are Trade Marks
of Usborne Publishing Ltd. All rights reserved. No part of this publication may be reproduced, stored in a retrieval system,
or transmitted in any form or by any means, electronic, mechanical, photocopying, recording or otherwise,
without the prior permission of the publisher. First published in America in 2006. UE. Printed in Dubai.